Italy Travel Guide

The Ultimate Guide to Travel to Italy on a

Cheap Budget

Sandy Rose

Table of Contents

Your Free Gift

I am really grateful and thankful for your purchase. As a small symbol of my appreciation, I would like to give you my FREE book on how to manage your time more efficiently to help you in your life.

In my time management ebook, you will find various ways and methods that will help you take control of your time and hence become more productive, so you can get more done in your day. You will also get all my new ebooks at a discounted price ☺

Here is the link for the ebook:
Download Now

Introduction

I want to thank you and congratulate you for downloading the book "Italy Travel Guide: The Ultimate Guide to Travel to Italy on a Cheap Budget".

This book contains proven steps and strategies on how to travel to Italy on a budget and enjoy the rich heritage of the beautiful country even on a shoestring budget.

Here's an inescapable fact: Italy is one of the top destinations in the world so no matter where you go, Italy has to be on your bucket list before you die. This book will help you live your dream with tried and tested rules of spending wisely in Italy while soaking in the rich tradition, history, food and culture.

If you do not learn how to spend your money wisely, you may land up spending a fortune when you can use that money in some other place. Read on to learn more about this ancient country of diverse landscapes, friendly people and delicious food. Italy beckons you to visit the lovely country as soon as possible!

Chapter 1: Italy – A Country with Beautiful Culture, Landscape, Art and Cuisine

Italy is not only a beautiful country but it is also full of ancient history, art and architecture. The life and culture of this magnificent country is nothing less than splendid. Whether you love their pasta, pizza, wine or the famous gelato, there is something for everyone. Italians love to live life to the fullest so if you choose Italy as your next vacation spot, be ready to dive in with them.

Italy is a safe country to visit without doubt, though occasional pickpocketing or scamming may occur in tourist areas. Italy is full of beautiful and affordable places to visit at least once in your life time. You can find beautiful Mediterranean beaches with incredible vistas. Just hike along the rugged mountains for free and enjoy the breathtaking views that you can never erase from your memory. Italy is also famous for its fiery volcanoes and of course, the museums that will take you many centuries behind. If you want to ski or just spend a romantic evening with your lover in a gondola ride in Venice, you have it all here. Italy should be on your bucket list no matter what you are looking for. This country will never let you down! Experience the aura of life here and take it back with you because Italy and the Italians are both very hard to forget!

Italy scores on the top destinations to travel around the world, especially for U.S. citizens. So you can amenities here that you can find at home. You will find comfort and luxury. The best places to visit in Italy, even on a budget, are:

- **Rome**

Rome is home to the iconic Vatican City, the Colosseum and many other ancient monuments. You cannot miss this city if you are visiting Italy. This is where religion and power takes over the world.

- **Florence & Tuscany**

Have you ever wondered where the Italian olive oil or the delicious Italian wine comes from? It is here in the Tuscany region of Italy. The rolling hills of the Tuscany region is dotted with cypress trees and olive garden. It is green wherever you see. Beautiful to watch and a relaxing experience for your eyes. Experience the incredible life at the vineyards and enjoy mouthwatering home-cooked food to build a lasting memory of Tuscany.

- **Venice**

Venice is an iconic romantic destination in the world. Although, you may land up spending a fortune on food if you are not careful, this city still has a lot to offer even when you are on a shoestring budget.

- **Pompeii**

With the fiery Mt. Vesuvius in the backdrop, this city has frozen since the eruption of the Vesuvius in 79 AD. Pompeii is a UNESCO World Heritage Site.

- **Cinque Terre**

The rugged and hauntingly gorgeous landscapes and views of the Mediterranean coast of Italy will leave you in awe and admiration. With the sinuous paths passing through the gigantic cliffs, Cinque Terre is also a UNESCO World Heritage Site and an authentic coastal town that has not changed much with time.

- **Naples**

Naples is home of the famous pizza! This city is famous for its delicious food and the Renaissance-era churches, castles and palaces. Naples is Italy's most luxurious, elegant and profound masterpiece that remains ageless since time unknown.

- **Verona**

Home to the start-crossed lovers, Romeo and Juliet, Verona is the ultimate romantic destination of today. With the Roman ruins, medieval castles and historic churches lying in the city, Verona has qualified to become a UNESCO World Heritage Site. Verona is also home to the famous 2000-year old Roman arena that hosts opera during summer.

- **Amalfi Coast**

The Amalfi Coast is where the rugged and breathtaking landscapes of the Mediterranean coast will take your breath away in an instant. You cannot stop drooling over this coastal gem with the picturesque towns and the lush green forests all around. It is simply magical and it will be sin to miss this experience!

Italy has so much to offer in every aspect, from fashion, food and luxury to religion, history and nature. Even when you are traveling on a shoestring budget, you can find ways to save and travel throughout this country that has so much to offer to all its visitors. You can also visit the less expensive cities and towns and still enjoy an authentic experience of Italy.

When to go?

Keep in mind that the peak tourist season in Italy runs from May to July. You can find good deals during the shoulder and off season. The cheapest time to travel to Italy is during winter, though Christmas can be expensive again. September and October has milder temperatures if you want to beat the heat. Ideally, if you want good deals and less crowd then August is a great time to travel to Italy, though temperatures can be a bit warm then.

Chapter 2: Travel in Italy on a Budget

If you want to grab good deals in airfare, try to travel during the off season. This way you can find good deals in airfare and accommodation in Italy. Another great way to find great deals in airfare is by traveling via cheaper European cities. Though Italian cities may be slightly more expensive, some of the other European cities may have better deals. You can look for budget airlines, trains or buses to commute from there to Italy. It may take you longer to reach Italy but if you are traveling on a budget, this could save you bucks. Budget airlines are good if you want to travel during the shoulder or off season. Prices may drop so you can avail this option. Try to find good deals with RyanAir or EasyJet. Make sure you read the baggage policy so you know if you have to pay for your check-in baggage. For booking your tickets, use the Italian websites, such as Mobissimo and Vayama. There are plenty of Italian carriers too that can help you with good deals.

Western Europe is well connected through land and though air. So don't miss out on the trains or buses if you get better deals. High speed trains may cost you around 40 to 70 Euros but you will reach Italy faster than other trains. Look at the brighter side, you get to see some beautiful countryside while traveling to Italy. Buses are cheap too. If you book well ahead of time, you may get discounts so keep an eye for them. Italy's train system is definitely cheaper than taking the plane or the car but beware of the train strikes which can be frustrating.

Even when you are commuting within Italy, you can still use trains and buses instead to travel from town to town. Enjoy the picturesque landscapes of rural Italy, a delight to watch, and something you will miss from a flight. Keep your cost low with some research and planned itinerary.

Avoid driving cars within the city because public transportation in Italy is affordable and efficient. Check the train schedules and keep the maps of the cities handy when you travel. The best way to explore a city is through walking. If you are visiting cities like Venice and Florence, walk as much as possible. You will see and hear a lot. Instead of wasting on a tour, just walk the town yourself. It may be intense, but you will see things you would miss otherwise. If you want more information about a city, you can stop by the tourist office. But, it is better if you research everything online beforehand to save time and confusion.

If you want to discover and enjoy the hill towns of Italy then you can rent a car. Usually renting a car costs around 40 to 60 Euros a day, so try to pack as many people as you can in a car to keep the cost down. Renting a car could be a good option for you when you are traveling with a group or with your family. The gas price may be around 5.87 Euros per gallon. If your car can get 35 miles per gallon then you are looking at 30 Euros for 165 miles (that is, the distance from Florence to Rome). So if you want to rent a car, then try to book beforehand to find some discounts and good deals. You can try to rent a car in smaller cities, like Florence, to get better deals and enjoy the Tuscany region from there. If you want to drop the car in another city, then pre-reserve this option to avail better rates. Italian driving may not be ideal so be aware of road accidents as that may cost you a lot.

Chapter 3: Accommodation in Italy on a Budget

If you want to get better deals in accommodation on a budget, then ditch the hotels. There are better ways to enjoy Italy even on a budget. After the airfare, accommodation takes a big slice of our budget. If you know where to look, you will find gorgeous deals to help you reduce that slice to a minimum.

You can look at short term room rentals on AirBnB and 9flats.com to find excellent deals for a room, an apartment or a cottage. As a single traveler you will need a room, private or shared. As a family you have the option to rent the entire apartment or cottage. This helps to keep your budget on a tight leash. If you don't mind staying at a private apartment and meet different people at your host's residence, then short term rental is the way to go.

You can also look for hostels if you don't mind sharing the room and bathroom with other people. You can also opt for a private room which may cost you more. Hostels are really good for short term travel because you land up saving more this way. If you are a backpacker or an unscheduled traveler, then this is the way to go. You may spend around 25 Euros a night for a bed in a shared room or around 90 Euros for your own room.

B&B is also a great way to strike a balance between the amenities of a hotel. It will be basic accommodation but with free breakfast and daily cleanings. It is usually more personal than a hotel and you will get to meet Italian families and other visitors this way. If you are planning to stay on the Amalfi Coast then look for B&B accommodations for an authentic Italian experience.

Have you heard of home exchange or watched the movie "The Holiday"? Swapping your house with another traveler is definitely a fun way to explore and experience each other's country and culture. You can become a member of the home exchange network to reap its benefits. This way you can stay away from tourist traps and enjoy the comfort of staying at home even when you are traveling abroad.

If you don't mind simple and austere surroundings, then you can also opt for religious housing. It is definitely an off-the-beaten-path to experience the life and culture in Italy. Find your choice of stay at Monastery Stays. Just make sure you return before the curfew or you may be locked out.

The choices are endless, depending on your budget. You can find something that will make your wallet happy. You can choose farm-stays or camping as long as it is fun for you or your family. Agriturismo or farm-stay is an excellent way to stay a day with animals around you. If you are traveling with children, then this will surely be an exciting stay for them. Usually you will spend around 50 Euros per person with food and stay. You can enjoy home-cooked meals and enjoy the gorgeous farms. Some of these accommodations can be luxurious too. Lots of open space and greenery is the way to go when you are traveling with children.

Chapter 4: Food in Italy on a Budget

Italy is famous for its culinary expertise and mouth-watering dishes. If you are on a strict budget then do keep in mind that any restaurant with a glass of wine will cost you 15 Euros or more. So make sure you read the menu before sitting down. One other thing is that some restaurants charge extra for a sitting down experience, so think before you sit! Some restaurants have special menu for lunch so you can make use of these deals. For dinner you can opt for pizza by the slice which can cost you about 3 to 5 Euros only.

The following budget food tips can help you survive in any Italian city:

- Try to adapt to the local culture and avoid caving for American or English breakfast for a while. For 3 Euros you can try the Italian breakfast that consists of a pastry and a cappuccino. It may not be filling but you can replenish the fiber and the vitamins with some fruits or fresh vegetables from a nearby food market.

- You can also buy breakfast food from the local grocery store and store it in your fridge (such as, milk, cereals, bread, etc.).

- You can have an elaborate and luxurious lunch for around 13 to 15 Euros. If you want to save, you can try the deli stores where you can find a sandwich for 3 Euros or more.

- Keep it simple. If you want to eat grilled veggies, keep in mind that it will be weighed so don't buy what you can't eat.

- If you are not a wine connoisseur, just stick with the house wine which will cost you around 6 to 10 Euros in a restaurant.

- Make sure you research well in advance. Some neighborhoods may be cheaper when compared to others. For instance, Sant'Ambrogio in Florence may offer cheaper options. So you can eat quality food for even less. Use Yelp to help you find local restaurants that match your budget, area and reviews.

- If you are traveling with a large group or family, try to save on exorbitant restaurant bills by doing picnic lunches in a beautiful park or garden. It is a beautiful experience that you cannot miss in Italy. In summer, you should carry a mosquito repellant too.

- If you have a sweet tooth, ditch the dessert at the restaurants and find a local gelato shop instead. They are usually open from 10 am until 1 am. You can get normal sized serving for around 2 to 3 Euros. You can also try some local favorites here that you can't miss!

- Having a pizza for dinner is a great option because you can find one for less than 10 Euros. Just try to pick a trattoria over an osteria. Trattorias are a great option if you want to enjoy a cozy, traditional and an authentic vibe of Italy. You will find fresh and conventional food here.

- You can fill your tummy with snacks that is readily available in a local food market, grocery store or roadside delis. As long as you don't give into temptation and stay away from the swanky "ristorante", you can keep a watch on your budget.

- Try the aperitivo in Italy. This will cost you about 10 Euros. You will receive an aperitif cocktail with a spread of snacks. This will keep your tummy on leash before you embark for dinner.

- When you go to a restaurant, ask for plain tap water, or what is known as acqua del rubinetto, since bottled water can be expensive. You will find drinking fountains throughout Italy so use it instead of buying bottled water.

- Instead of buying wine at the restaurants, buy wine at grocery stores for just 4 Euros. Save the extra money to do something else instead.

- Some restaurants in Italy may also charge you extra for bread or breadsticks on the table. They may not tell you and you will be surprised when the check comes. So find out if your bread is charged before you bite it!

If you eat like a local, or buy from local food markets and make your own breakfast, you will definitely cut down on the extra cost of buying meals every time. There are plenty of local cafes in Italy so make the most of it and stay away from seemingly-nice tourist traps. They will offer you great views but the food may not be great. So, keeping all this in mind, head out and enjoy Italy!

Chapter 5: Top Things to Do in Italy on a Budget

- Like most of the other cities, try to take Walking Tours in Italy to go easy on your wallet. If you are staying in a hostel, then find out more about these affordable tours. You may also find free walking tours where you just need to tip the guide instead of paying for the entire tour.

- Some museums may offer free entrance on certain day of the week. Find out about it and try to beat the crowd early and enjoy the museum at no cost.

- Another interesting way of exploring a city is by renting a bike. It is pretty popular with tourists and you can cover more grounds than by foot. You will find plenty of good deals for 15 Euros or less per day.

- If you want to travel to the coastal regions like the Amalfi Coast or Cinque Terra, then you can consider hiking the mountains to get ravishing views of the landscape. It is like a bird's eye view of the Mediterranean coast. The dramatic coastline with plunging mountains and perilous cliffsides will keep you wanting for more. It may take some time but if you don't have to worry about that, then this is a definite thing to experience, plus it is free!

- Try to go to Venice during the Venice Carnival. It is ten days of unstoppable fun, masquerade and lasting nights of dancing and drinking. It is inexplicable and you need to experience it for yourself!

- Venice is a beautiful city beyond words. Beside the Carnival, there is one more reason to fall in love with this amazing city, the Gondola ride. You have to experience the gondola ride and a romantic candlelight dinner in Venice at least once in your life time. Though Venice is not an affordable city, but it is beautiful and a definite to-do on your bucket list! You can also enjoy the rich history, art and culture of Venice by just visiting the churches and basilicas for free, such as the St. Mark's Basilica.

- If you go to Italy, don't miss out on the ruins in Pompeii. This city has stood still since the Mt. Vesuvius exploded. Experience the day when the fury of the volcano took over the normal lives of this ancient city. It is definitely a full day activity for you.

- If you want to enjoy the hills and the beautiful wine region of Italy, then Tuscany is the way to go. Rent a car if you can afford it and get lost in the undulating landscapes and the olive gardens dotting the hills of this region. Enjoy home-cooked fresh meals and take back the lovely memories of Italy with you. Take wine tours.

- Stop at Florence and enjoy some mouth-watering and delicious gelato. Enjoy the beautiful city from Piazzale Michelangelo.

- Rome is a very special place and everyone who visits Italy has to experience the history and the present religion power at Rome. You will definitely need more than one trip to delve into the history of Rome. If you want to enjoy some cheap food, go to Trastevere which is a student neighborhood. It is located west of the river and has great bars and tiny streets that tourists love to crawl into. You can choose to just relax in Villa Borghese Park or watch the sunset from Piazza del Campidoglio. This experience will leave you speechless!

- A visit to Rome is not complete without spending time browsing through the rich history of the Vatican museums. You will find long lines here so try to be early and be patient. Your patience will be truly rewarded!

- You cannot miss visiting Rome especially during Christmas. The Christmas market in Rome is famous all over the world!

- Cinque Terra is a beautiful town. You will feel like time has stopped here. The picturesque houses along with the landscape has been preserved beyond doubt. Enjoy the fresh pesto and the mouth-watering seafood along with the local wine. It will make your trip undoubtedly the best! Each city here has its own vibe so visit them all to get the best experience.

- Italy is famous for its mountains and rugged coastline. Italy is also home to Lake Como. The beautiful lakes up north are very busy during the summer. You will find rich Italians here. So just sit, relax and enjoy the beautiful villas around the lake. You may also catch a glimpse of George Clooney.

- Sicily is an interesting place to visit. Though it is famous for its mafia, the island also has its own local delicacies that you can enjoy. Also, the beaches are warm in the summer so if you are beach bummer then Sicily is the way to go.

- Alberobello is a very cute town in Southern Italy. It is a UNESCO World Heritage Site and a great place to visit between November to April. You can also find great bars and restaurants all over this town.

Italy is famous for its rich history, delicious cuisines and great people. Your life is not complete until you make your way up to this great destination. Whether it is the vineyards in Florence, the gorgeous cliffs in Cinque Terra, the romantic gondola rides in Venice or the relaxed life of the people in Southern Italy, you will find plenty to make your trip to Italy memorable. Don't rush! Relax and enjoy the country with a panini and a latte.

Conclusion

Thank you again for downloading this book!

I truly hope this book helped you understand how to plan an idea vacation in Italy on a shoestring budget.

Your next step is to set up your calendar and finding your first available dates to plan your ultimate vacation in Italy.

Thank you and good luck!

Your Free Gift

I am really grateful and thankful for your purchase. As a small symbol of my appreciation, I would like to give you my FREE book on how to manage your time more efficiently to help you in your life.

In my time management ebook, you will find various ways and methods that will help you take control of your time and hence become more productive, so you can get more done in your day. You will also get all my new ebooks at a discounted price ☺

Here is the link for the ebook:
Download Now

Printed in the USA
CPSIA information can be obtained
at www.ICGtesting.com
LVHW012245080624
782712LV00010B/808